contents

Hoosier Block Afghan	2
Yipes Stripes Afghan	5
Math Geek Afghan	8
Winding Road Afghan	11
Windy City Afghan	14
Land of Lincoln Afghan	16
Monday's Child Afghan	20
Homegrown Afghan	22
November Nights Afghan	24
Country Colors Afghan	27
City Block Afghan	30

For pattern inquiries, please visit: www.go-crafty.com

hoosier block afghan

YARN
- Lion Brand® HOMESPUN® THICK & QUICK® (Art. #792)
- 1 skein #312 Edwardian (A)
- 1 skein #404 Lagoon (B)
- 2 skeins #412 Pearls (C)
- 2 skeins #411 Mixed Berries (D)
- 1 skein #436 Claret (E) or colors of your choice

HOOK
- Lion Brand® crochet hook size N/13 (9 mm) or size to obtain gauge

NOTIONS
- Lion Brand® large-eyed blunt needle

FINISHED MEASUREMENTS
About 44 x 48 in. (112 x 122 cm)

GAUGE
6 half double crochet (hdc) and 4 rows = 4 in. (10 cm).
BE SURE TO CHECK YOUR GAUGE.

When you match the gauge in a pattern, your project will be the size specified in the pattern and the materials specified in the pattern will be sufficient. If it takes you fewer stitches and rows to match the gauge, try using a smaller size hook; if more stitches and rows, try a larger size hook.

NOTES
1. 7 Strips are worked, each following a Stripe Sequence. Strips are sewn together to make the Afghan.
2. Border is crocheted around the outside edge of the completed Afghan.
3. To change color, work last st of old color to last yarn over. Yarn over with new color and draw through all loops to complete the stitch. Fasten off old color.
4. We used almost every bit of yarn in this project! Be sure not to leave overly long yarn tails and if necessary, use scrap yarn to sew the Strips together.

STRIP 1
Strip 1 Stripe Sequence Work 2 rows with D, 4 rows A, 2 rows B, 4 rows E, 2 rows A, 4 rows C, 4 rows D, 2 rows A, 2 rows C, 4 rows B, 6 rows C, 4 rows E, 2 rows D, 2 rows B, 2 rows C, 4 rows A.

With first color in Stripe Sequence, chain 11.
Row 1 Half double crochet in 3rd chain from hook (beginning chain does not count as a stitch) and in each chain across—9 half double crochet.
Row 2 Chain 2 (does not count as a stitch), turn, half double crochet in each stitch across. Repeat Row 2, changing color following Stripe Sequence until all 50 rows are complete. Fasten off.

STRIPS 2–7
Work same as Strip 1, in the following Stripe Sequences.

Strip 2 Stripe Sequence Work 4 rows with C, 4 rows E, 2 rows D, 2 rows B, 2 rows C, 4 rows A, 2 rows D, 4 rows A, 2 rows B, 4 rows E, 2 rows A, 4 rows C, 4 rows D, 2 rows A, 2 rows C, 4 rows B, 2 rows C.

Strip 3 Stripe Sequence Work 4 rows with E, 2 rows A, 4 rows C, 4 rows D, 2 rows A, 2 rows C, 4 rows B, 6 rows C, 4 rows E, 2 rows D, 2 rows B, 2 rows C, 4 rows A, 2 rows D, 4 rows A, 2 rows B.

Strip 4 Stripe Sequence Work 4 rows with A, 2 rows D, 4 rows A, 2 rows B, 4 rows E, 2 rows A, 4 rows C, 4 rows D, 2 rows A, 2 rows C, 4 rows B, 6 rows C, 4 rows E, 2 rows D, 2 rows B, 2 rows C.

Strip 5 Stripe Sequence Work 2 rows with A, 2 rows C, 4 rows B, 6 rows C, 4 rows E, 2 rows D, 2 rows B, 2 rows C, 4 rows A, 2 rows D, 4 rows A, 2 rows B, 4 rows E, 2 rows A, 4 rows C, 4 rows D.

hoosier block afghan

Strip 6 Stripe Sequence Work 2 rows with D, 2 rows B, 2 rows C, 4 rows A, 2 rows D, 4 rows A, 2 rows B, 4 rows E, 2 rows A, 4 rows C, 4 rows D, 2 rows A, 2 rows C, 4 rows B, 6 rows C, 4 rows E.

Strip 7 Stripe Sequence Work 2 rows with B, 4 rows E, 2 rows A, 4 rows C, 4 rows D, 2 rows A, 2 rows C, 4 rows B, 6 rows C, 4 rows E, 2 rows D, 2 rows B, 2 rows C, 4 rows A, 2 rows D, 4 rows A.

FINISHING
Sew long edges of Strips together in numerical order.

Border
From right side, join D with a slip stitch anywhere along outer edge of Afghan.

Rnd 1 Chain 1, single crochet (sc) evenly spaced around entire outer edge of Afghan, working 3 single crochet in each corner; join with slip stitch in first single crochet.

Rnd 2 Chain 1, single crochet in each stitch around, working 3 single crochet in each corner; join with slip stitch in first single crochet. Fasten off.
Weave in ends.

yipes stripes afghan

YARN
Lion Brand® HOMESPUN® (Art. #790)
- 4 skeins #381 Barley (A)
- 3 skeins #412 Pearls (B)
- 3 skeins #311 Rococo (C) or colors of your choice

HOOK
- Lion Brand® crochet hook size K/10.5 (6.5 mm) *or size to obtain gauge*

NOTIONS
- Lion Brand® large-eyed blunt needle

ABBREVIATIONS
beg = beginning
ch = chain
ch-sp = space previously made
hdc = half double crochet
rep = repeat
RS = right side
rnd = round
sc = single crochet
sk = skip
sl st = slip stitch
st(s) = stitch(es)
WS = wrong side

FINISHED MEASUREMENTS
About 39 x 49 in. (99 x 124.5 cm)

GAUGE
8 sc and 13 rows = 4 in. (10 cm).
BE SURE TO CHECK YOUR GAUGE.

When you match the gauge in a pattern, your project will be the size specified in the pattern and the materials specified in the pattern will be sufficient. If it takes you fewer stitches and rows to match the gauge, try using a smaller size hook; if more stitches and rows, try a larger size hook.

NOTES
1 Afghan is worked diagonally, from corner to corner, in a Stripe Sequence.
2 To change color when working Stripe Sequence, work last st of old color to last yarn over. Yarn over with new color and draw through all loops to complete st. Fasten off old color.
3 Work all sc2tog over the next 2 sts whether they are 2 hdc, 2 sc, or 1 hdc and 1 ch-1 sp.
4 When instructed to work in each st across, work in each st and in each ch-1 sp (if any) of previous row.
5 Some rows are worked as both right side rows and wrong side rows. Be sure to keep track of which row you are on!

STITCH GLOSSARY
sc2tog (sc 2 sts together) (Insert hook in next st and draw up a loop) twice, yarn over and draw through all 3 loops on hook—1 st decreased.

sc3tog (sc 3 sts together) (Insert hook in next st and draw up a loop) 3 times, yarn over and draw through all 4 loops on hook—2 sts decreased.

STRIPE SEQUENCE
Work *10 rows with A, 5 rows with B, 7 rows with C; rep from * for Stripe Sequence.

AFGHAN
With C, ch 2.
Row 1 Work 3 sc in 2nd ch from hook—3 sts at the end of this row.
Row 2 Ch 1, turn, 2 sc in first st, sc in each st across to last st, 2 sc in last st—5 sts.
Row 3 Rep Row 2—7 sts.
Row 4 Ch 1, turn, hdc in first st, *ch 1, sk next st, hdc in next st; rep from * to end of row—4 hdc and 3 ch-1 sps.
Change to A and beg Stripe Sequence.
Continue changing color as in Stripe Sequence to end of work.
Rows 5–8 Rep Row 2—15 sts at the end of Row 8.

5

yipes stripes afghan

Row 9 Rep Row 4—8 hdc and 7 ch-1 sps.
Rep Rows 5–9, following Stripe Sequence, until piece measures 38 in. (96.5 cm) from beg, measured across a side edge, end with a Row 9.
Note End with a Row 9 means that the last row you work should be a Row 9.

SECOND CORNER

Row 1 Ch 1, turn, sc2tog, sc in each st across to last st, 2 sc in last st.
Row 2 Ch 1, turn, 2 sc in first st, sc in each st across to last 2 sts, sc2tog.
Rows 3 and 4 Rep Rows 1 and 2.
Row 5 Ch 1, turn, hdc in first st, *ch 1, sk next st, hdc in next st; rep from * to last st, hdc in last st.
Rep Rows 1–5 until piece measures 48 in. (122 cm) measured across longest side edge, end with a Row 5.

THIRD AND FOURTH CORNERS

Row 1 Sc2tog, sc in each st across to last 2 sts, sc2tog.
Rows 2–4 Rep Row 1 three times.
Row 5 Ch 1, turn, hdc in first st, *ch 1, sk next st, hdc in next st; rep from * to end of row.
Rep Rows 1–5 until 3 sts remain.
Last Row Ch 1, turn, sc3tog.
Fasten off.

FINISHING
Border

Rnd 1 From RS, join A with sl st anywhere along outside edge of Afghan. Work sc evenly spaced all the way around outside edge, working 3 sc in each corner; join with sl st in first st.
Rnd 2 Ch 1, turn, sc in each st around, working 3 sc in each corner; join with sl st in first sc. Fasten off.
Weave in ends.

math geek afghan

YARN (5)
Lion Brand® HOMESPUN® (Art. #790)
- 2 skeins #311 Rococo (A)
- 2 skeins #386 Grape (B)
- 2 skeins #375 Candy Apple 2 (C)
- 1 skein #368 Montana Sky (D) or colors of your choice

HOOK
- Lion Brand® crochet hook size K/10.5 (6.5 mm) *or size to obtain gauge*

NOTIONS
- Lion Brand® large-eyed blunt needle

ABBREVIATIONS
beg = beginning
ch = chain
ch-sp = space previously made
dc = double crochet
rep = repeat
RS = right side
rnd(s) = round(s)
sc = single crochet
sl st = slip stitch
sp(s) = space(s)
st(s) = stitch(es)
WS = wrong side

FINISHED MEASUREMENTS
About 40 x 46 in. (101.5 x 117 cm)

GAUGE
One Hexagon measures about 10 in. (25.5 cm) across.
BE SURE TO CHECK YOUR GAUGE.

When you match the gauge in a pattern, your project will be the size specified in the pattern and the materials specified in the pattern will be sufficient. If it takes you fewer stitches and rows to match the gauge, try using a smaller size hook; if more stitches and rows, try a larger size hook.

NOTES
1 Afghan is made from 18 Hexagons and 4 Half Hexagons.
2 Hexagons are worked in joined rnds with RS facing at all times, changing color every other rnd.
3 Half Hexagons are worked back and forth in rows, changing color every other row.
4 Hexagons and Half Hexagons are arranged as shown in Assembly Diagram, then crocheted together. Border is worked around outer edge of Afghan.

HEXAGON #1 (MAKE 8)
With C, ch 4; join with sl st in first ch to form a ring.
Rnd 1 (RS) Ch 5 (counts as dc + ch 2 in this rnd and in all following rnds), (3 dc in ring, ch 2) 5 times, 2 dc in ring; join with sl st in 3rd ch of beg ch—18 dc and 6 ch-2 sps at the end of this rnd.
Rnd 2 (Sl st, ch 5, dc) in first ch-sp, *dc in next 3 dc, (dc, ch 2, dc) in next ch-2 sp; rep from * 4 more times, dc in last 3 dc; join with sl st in 3rd ch of ch—30 dc and 6 ch-2 sps. Fasten off.
Rnd 3 With RS facing, join A with sl st in any ch-2 sp, ch 5, dc in same ch-sp, *dc in each dc to next ch-2 sp, (dc, ch 2, dc) in next ch-2 sp; rep from * 4 more times, dc in each dc to end of rnd; join with sl st in 3rd ch of beg ch—42 dc and 6 ch-2 sps.
Rnd 4 (Sl st, ch 5, dc) in first ch-sp, *dc in each dc to next ch-2 sp, (dc, ch 2, dc) in next ch-2 sp; rep from * 4 more times, dc in each dc to end of rnd; join with sl st in 3rd ch of beg ch—54 dc and 6 ch-2 sps. Fasten off.
Rnds 5 and 6 With B, rep Rnds 3 and 4—78 dc and 6 ch-2 sps at the end of Rnd 6. Fasten off.

HEXAGON #2 (MAKE 5)
Make same as Hexagon #1, working in the following color sequence: work Rnds 1 and 2 with A, work Rnds 3 and 4 with B, work Rnds 5 and 6 with C.

HEXAGON #3 (MAKE 5)
Make same as Hexagon #1, working in the following color sequence: work Rnds 1 and 2 with B, work Rnds 3 and 4 with C, work Rnds 5 and 6 with A.

HALF HEXAGON #1 (MAKE 2)
With A, ch 3; join with sl st in first ch to form a ring.
Row 1 (RS) Ch 3 (counts as dc in this row and in all following rows), 2 dc in ring, (ch 2, 3 dc in ring) 2 times—9 dc and 2 ch-2 sps at the end of this row.
Row 2 Ch 3, turn, dc in first dc (increase made), dc in next 2 dc, *(dc, ch 2, dc) in next ch-2 sp, dc in next 3 dc; rep from * once more, dc once more in last dc (increase made)—15 dc and 2 ch-2 sps at the end of this row. Fasten off.
Row 3 With RS facing, join B with sl st in first dc, ch 3, dc in same st as join, *dc in each dc to next ch-2 sp, (dc, ch 2, dc) in next ch-2 sp; rep from * once more, dc in each dc to turning ch, 2 dc in top of turning ch—21 dc and 2 ch-2 sps at the end of this row.
Row 4 Ch 3, turn, dc in same st as join, *dc in each dc to next ch-2 sp, (dc, ch 2, dc) in next ch-2 sp; rep from * once more, dc in each dc to turning ch, 2 dc in top of turning ch—27 dc and 2 ch-2 sps at the end of this row. Fasten off.
Rows 5 and 6 With C, rep Rows 3 and 4—39 dc and 2 ch-2 sps. Fasten off.

math geek afghan

HALF HEXAGON #2 (MAKE 2)
Make same as Half Hexagon #1, working in the following color sequence: work Rows 1 and 2 with B, work Rows 3 and 4 with C, work Rows 5 and 6 with A.

FINISHING
Arrange Hexagons and Half Hexagons as shown in Assembly Diagram.
From WS, join D with sl st at edge between 2 pieces. Working through edges of both pieces, sc across to join pieces. Join remaining pieces in the same way.

Border
Rnd 1 With RS facing, join D with sc anywhere in outer edge of Afghan, sc evenly spaced around entire outer edge; join with sl st in first sc.
Fasten off.
Weave in ends.

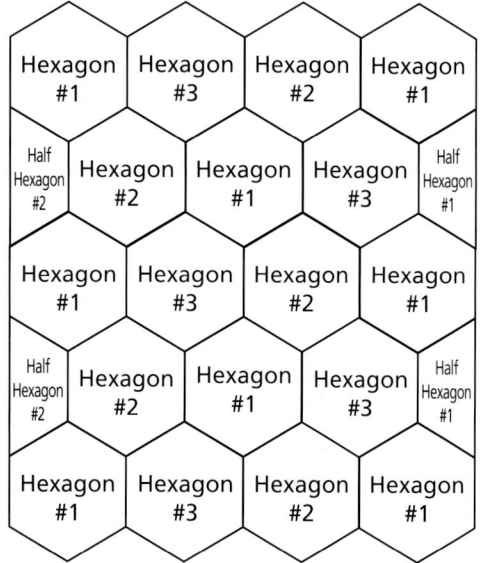

winding road afghan

YARN
Lion Brand® HOMESPUN® (Art. #790)
- 4 skeins #419 Tumbleweed (A)
- 2 skeins #408 Wild Fire (B)
- 3 skeins #318 Sierra (C) or colors of your choice

HOOK
- Lion Brand® crochet hook size K/10.5 (6.5 mm) *or size to obtain gauge*

NOTIONS
- Lion Brand® stitch marker
- Lion Brand® large-eyed blunt needle

ABBREVIATIONS
ch = chain
hdc = half double crochet
rnd(s) = round(s)
RS = right side
sc = single crochet
sl st = slip stitch
st(s) = stitch(es)
tog = together
WS = wrong side

FINISHED MEASUREMENTS
About 36 x 52 in. (91.5 x 132 cm)

GAUGE
9 sc and 12 rows = 4 in. (10 cm).
BE SURE TO CHECK YOUR GAUGE.

When you match the gauge in a pattern, your project will be the size specified in the pattern and the materials specified in the pattern will be sufficient. If it takes you fewer stitches and rows to match the gauge, try using a smaller size hook; if more stitches and rows, try a larger size hook.

STITCH GLOSSARYS
sc3tog (sc 3 sts together) (Insert hook in next st and draw up a loop) 3 times, yarn and draw through all 4 loops on hook—2 sts decreased.

sc5tog (sc 5 sts together) (Insert hook in next st and draw up a loop) 5 times, yarn over and draw through all 6 loops on hook—4 sts decreased.

NOTES
1 Afghan is made from 6 Squares, each worked in a different color sequence.
2 Each Square is worked back and forth in rows with a decrease worked at the center of each row to form the miter.
3 Squares are sewn together to make the Afghan.
4 Border is crocheted around the outside edge of the completed Afghan.
5 To change color, work last st of old color to last yarn over. Yarn over with new color and draw through all loops to complete the st. Fasten off old color.

SQUARE I
With A, ch 76.
Row 1 (WS) Sc in 2nd ch from hook and in next 35 ch, sc3tog, place marker in st just completed, sc in last 36 ch—73 sts at the end of this row.
Rows 2 and 3 Ch 1, turn, sc in each st to 1 st before marker, sc3tog, move marker to st just completed, sc in each st to end of row—69 sts at the end of Row 3.
Row 4 Ch 1, turn, sc in each st across.
Rows 5–7 Rep Row 2 three times—63 sts at the end of Row 7.
Rows 8–15 Rep Rows 4–7 twice—51 sts at the end of Row 15.
Row 16 Rep Row 4; change to C in last st.
Rows 17–19 With C, rep Row 2 three times—45 sts at the end of Row 19.
Rows 20–31 With C, rep Rows 4–7 three times—27 sts at the end of Row 31.
Row 32 With C, rep Row 4; change to A in last st.
Rows 33–35 With A, rep Row 2 three times—21 sts at the end of Row 35.
Rows 36–43 With A, rep Rows 4–7 twice—9 sts at the end of Row 43.
Row 44 With A, rep Row 4.
Rows 45 and 46 With A, rep Row 2 twice—5 sts at the end of Row 46.
Row 47 Ch 1, turn, sc5tog. Fasten off.

winding road afghan

SQUARE II
Work same as Square I, in following color sequence: Work Rows 1–16 with C, Rows 17–32 with A, and Rows 33–47 with B.

SQUARE III
Work same as Square I, in following color sequence: Work Rows 1–16 with A, Rows 17–32 with B, and Rows 33–47 with C.

SQUARE IV
Work same as Square I, in following color sequence: Work Rows 1–16 with A, Rows 17–32 with B, and Rows 33–47 with C.

SQUARE V
Work same as Square I, in following color sequence: Work Rows 1–16 with B, Rows 17–32 with C, and Rows 33–47 with B.

SQUARE VI
Work same as Square I, in following color sequence: Work Rows 1–16 with C, Rows 17–32 with A, and Rows 33–47 with B.

FINISHING
Following Assembly Diagram, sew Squares into 2 strips of 3 Squares each. Sew strips tog to make Afghan.

Border
Rnd 1 From RS, join C with sl st in any corner, ch 1, hdc evenly spaced around entire outer edge of Afghan, working 3 hdc in each corner; join with sl st in first st. Fasten off. From RS, join B with sl st in any corner.
Rnds 2–4 With B, ch 1, sc in each st around, working 3 sc in each corner; join with sl st in first sc.
Fasten off.
Weave in ends.

Assembly Diagram

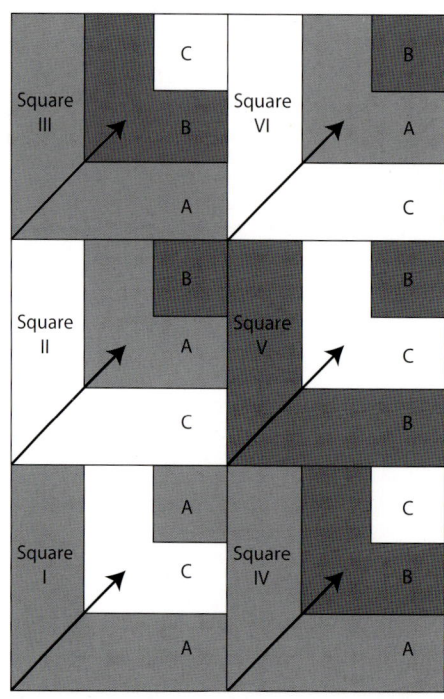

A = #419 Tumbleweed
B = #408 Wild Fire
C = #318 Sierra

windy city afghan

YARN
Lion Brand® HOMESPUN® (Art. #790)
- 2 skeins #302 Colonial (A)
- 2 skeins #341 Windsor (B)
- 2 skein #412 Pearls (C)
- 1 skein #386 Grape (D)
- 1 skein #399 Apple Green (E)
- 2 skeins #375 Candy Apple (F)
- 2 skeins #394 Golden (G) or colors of your choice

NEEDLES
- Lion Brand® crochet hook size K/10.5 (6.5 mm) or size to obtain gauge

NOTIONS
- Lion Brand® large-eyed blunt needle

ABBREVIATIONS
ch = chain
hdc = half double crochet
rnd(s) = round(s)
sl st = slip stitch
st(s) = stitch(es)

FINISHED MEASUREMENTS
About 46 x 46 in. (117 x 117 cm)

GAUGES
- 10 hdc and 8 rows = 4 in. (10 cm).
- One Block measures about 5 x 5 in. (12.5 x 12.5 cm).

BE SURE TO CHECK YOUR GAUGES.

When you match the gauge in a pattern, your project will be the size specified in the pattern and the materials specified in the pattern will be sufficient. If it takes you fewer stitches and rows to match the gauge, try using a smaller hook; if more stitches and rows, try a larger hook.

NOTES
1 Afghan is made from 81 Blocks. Blocks are identical except for color.
2 Following Assembly Diagram, Blocks are turned in different directions and then sewn together.
3 Border is crocheted around the outside edge of the completed Afghan.

AFGHAN
Block (make 81—16 with A, 4 with B, 12 with C, 4 with D, 12 with E, 17 with F, and 16 with G)
Ch 14.
Row 1 Hdc in 3rd ch from hook (beginning ch does not count as a st) and in each ch across—12 sts at the end of this row.
Rows 2–10 Ch 2 (does not count as a st), turn, hdc in each st across. Fasten off.

FINISHING
Following Assembly Diagram, sew Blocks into 9 strips of 9 Blocks each. Sew strips together to make Afghan.

Border
Rnd 1 From right side, join B with sl st anywhere along outside edge of Afghan, sl st evenly around outside edge of Afghan; join with sl st in first sl st.
Rnd 2 Ch 2, hdc in each st around, working 3 hdc in each corner; join with sl st in first hdc. Fasten off.
Weave in ends.

Assembly Diagram

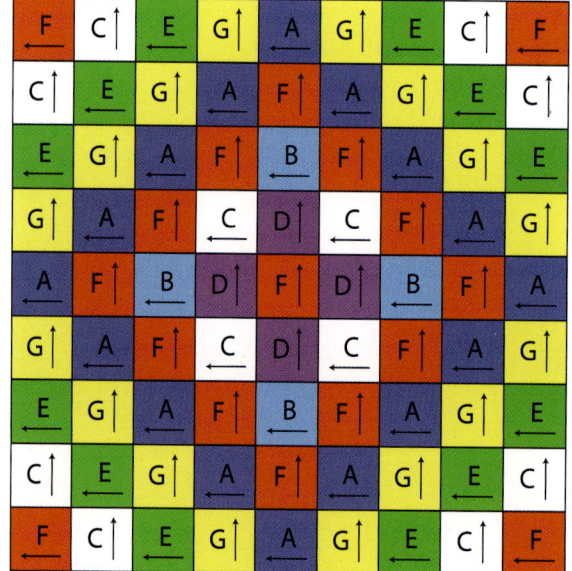

Note: Arrow is drawn from first row to last row of Block.

- #302 Colonial (A)
- #341 Windsor (B)
- #412 Pearls (C)
- #386 Grape (D)
- #399 Apple Green (E)
- #375 Candy Apple (F)
- #394 Golden (G)

land of lincoln afghan

YARN
Lion Brand® HOMESPUN® (Art. #790)
- 4 skeins #419 Tumbleweed (A)
- 2 skeins #408 Wild Fire (B)
- 3 skeins #318 Sierra (C) or colors of your choice

HOOK
- Lion Brand® crochet hook size K/10.5 (6.5 mm) or size to obtain gauge

NOTIONS
- Lion Brand® large-eyed blunt needle

ABBREVIATIONS
ch = chain
hdc = half double crochet
rnd(s) = round(s)
RS = right side
sc = single crochet
sl st = slip stitch
st(s) = stitch(es)
tog = together
WS = wrong side

FINISHED MEASUREMENTS
About 55 x 55 in. (139.5 x 139.5 cm)

GAUGES
- 10 sc and 12 rows = 4 in. (10 cm).
- Each Square measures about 6½ x 6½ in. (16.5 x 16.5 cm).

BE SURE TO CHECK YOUR GAUGES.

When you match the gauge in a pattern, your project will be the size specified in the pattern and the materials specified in the pattern will be sufficient. If it takes you fewer stitches and rows to match the gauge, try using a smaller hook; if more stitches and rows, try a larger hook.

NOTES
1. Afghan is made from 64 identical Squares which are made up of a Center Square and color bands referred to as Logs.
2. 16 Squares are sewn together to make a Block; then Blocks are sewn together to make the Afghan.
3. A diagram for the Square is provided for ease in construction.
4. The Border is worked around the outside edge of the completed Afghan.
5. To change color, work last st of old color to last yarn over. Yarn over with new color and draw through all loops to complete st. Fasten off old color.

SQUARE (MAKE 64)
Center Square
With A, ch 7.
Row 1 (RS) Sc in 2nd ch from hook and in each ch across—6 sc at the end of this row.
Rows 2–6 Ch 1, turn, sc in each sc across. Change to B in last st of last row.

First Log
Rows 1–3 With B, ch 1, turn, sc in each sc across.
Note The Log should measure about 1 in. (2.5 cm) wide. Do not fasten off.

Second Log
Second Log is worked across short end of First Log and next edge of Center Square.
Row 1 (RS) With B, ch 1, do not turn, work 3 sc evenly spaced across short end of First Log, and 6 sc across edge of Center Square—9 sc.
Rows 2 and 3 Ch 1, turn, sc in each sc across. Change to C in last st of last row. Fasten off B.

Third Log
Note Third Log is worked across short end of Second Log and next side of Center Square.
Row 1 (RS) With C, ch 1, do not turn, work 3 sc evenly spaced across short end of Second Log, and 6 sc across edge of Center Square—9 sc.
Rows 2 and 3 Ch 1, turn, sc in each sc across. Do not fasten off.

Fourth Log
Fourth Log is worked across short end of Third Log, last side of Center square and short end of First Log.
Row 1 (RS) With C, ch 1, do not turn, work 3 sc evenly spaced across short end of Third Log, 6 sc across last edge of Center Square, and 3 sc across short end of First Log—12 sc.
Rows 2 and 3 Ch 1, turn, sc in each sc across. Change to D in last st of last row. Fasten off C.

Fifth Log
Fifth Log is worked across short end of Fourth Log, long edge of First Log and short end of Second Log.
Row 1 (RS) With D, ch 1, do not turn, work 3 sc evenly spaced across short end of Fourth Log, 6 sc across long edge of First Log, and 3 sc across short end of Second Log—12 sc.
Rows 2 and 3 Ch 1, turn, sc in each sc across. Do not fasten off.

Sixth Log
Sixth Log is worked across short end of Fifth Log, long edge of Second Log and short end of Third Log.
Row 1 (RS) With D, ch 1, do not turn, work 3 sc evenly spaced across short end of Fifth Log,

land of lincoln afghan

9 sc across long edge of Second Log, and 3 sc across short end of Third Log—15 sc.
Rows 2 and 3 Ch 1, turn, sc in each sc across.
Change to E in last st of last row. Fasten off D.

Seventh Log
Seventh Log is worked across short end of Sixth Log, long edge of Third Log and short end of Fourth Log.
Row 1 (RS) With E, ch 1, do not turn, work 3 sc evenly spaced across short end of Sixth Log, 9 sc across long edge of Third Log, and 3 sc across short end of Fourth Log—15 sc.
Rows 2 and 3 Ch 1, turn, sc in each sc across. Do not fasten off.

Eighth Log
Eighth Log is worked across short end of Seventh Log, long edge of Fourth Log and short end of Fifth Log.
Row 1 (RS) With E, ch 1, do not turn, work 3 sc evenly spaced across short end of Seventh Log, 12 sc across long edge of Fourth Log, and 3 sc across short end of Fifth Log—18 sc.
Rows 2 and 3 Ch 1, turn, sc in each sc across. Fasten off E.

FINISHING
Following Block Assembly Diagram, arrange 16 Squares into 4 rows of 4 Squares each. Sew Squares together to make Block. Make 4 Blocks. Following Afghan Assembly Diagram, sew Blocks together to make Afghan.

Border
Note Work the Border VERY loosely.
Rnd 1 (RS) With C, join yarn with sl st anywhere along outside edge of Afghan, ch 3 (counts as first dc here and throughout), dc evenly spaced around outside edge, working 3 dc in each corner; join with sl st in top of beg ch.
Rnd 2 Ch 3, dc in each dc around, working 3 dc in each corner; join with sl st in top of beg ch. Fasten off.
Weave in ends.

Assembly Diagram

64 Squares (4 Blocks) Arranged into Afghan

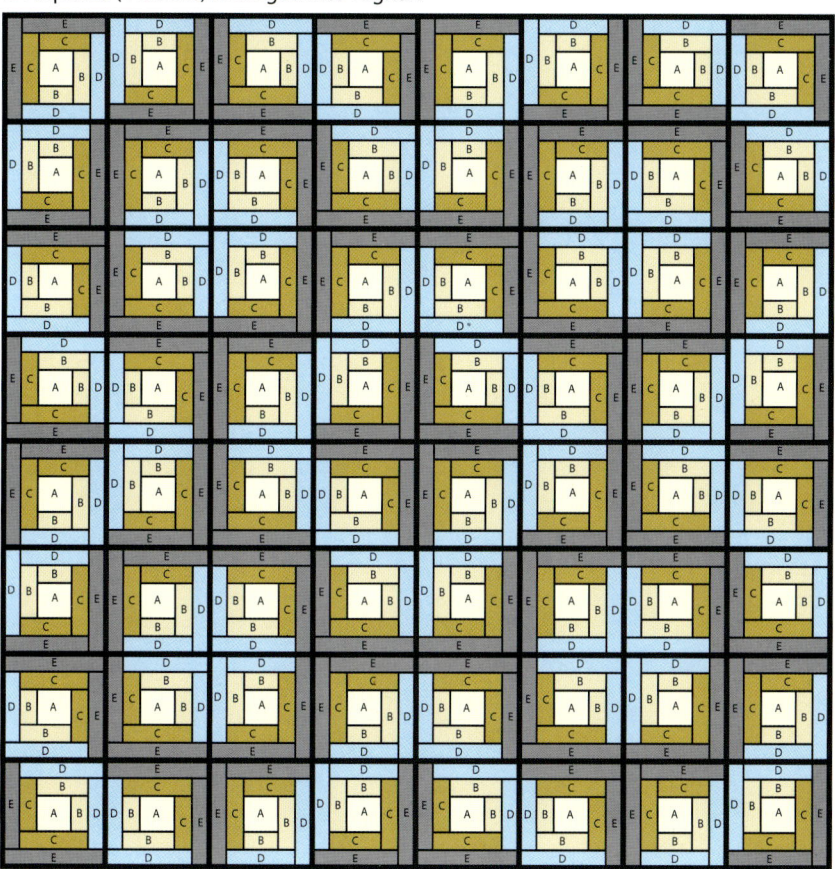

16 Squares Arranged into one Block

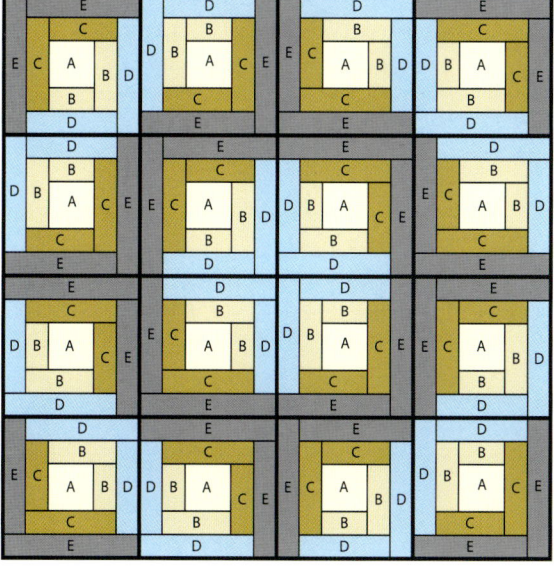

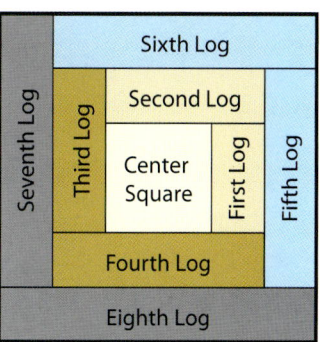

- #412 Pearls (A)
- #311 Rococo (B)
- #381 Barley (C)
- #320 Regency (D)
- #312 Edwardian (E)

monday's child afghan

YARN
Lion Brand® HOMESPUN® (Art. #792)
- 3 skeins #412 Pearls (A)
- 3 skeins #381 Barley (B)
- 3 skeins #407 Painted Desert (C) or colors of your choice

HOOK
- Lion Brand® crochet hook size P/15 (10 mm) *or size to obtain gauge*

NOTIONS
- Lion Brand® large-eyed blunt needle

FINISHED MEASUREMENTS
About 56 x 64 in. (142 x 162.5 cm)

GAUGE
6 half double crochet (hdc) and 5 rows = about 4 in. (10 cm).
BE SURE TO CHECK YOUR GAUGE.

When you match the gauge in a pattern, your project will be the size specified in the pattern and the materials specified in the pattern will be sufficient. If it takes you fewer stitches to match the gauge, try using a smaller size hook or needles; if more stitches, try a larger size hook or needles.

NOTES
1. Four Panels are worked separately, then sewn together to make Throw.
2. The color is changed every 16 rows on each Panel.
3. To change color, work last stitch of old color to last yarn over. Yarn over with new color and draw through all loops on hook to complete the stitch. Fasten off old color.
4. The chain 2 at the beginning of every row is a turning chain and does not count as a stitch.

PANEL I
With A, chain 23.
Row 1 Half double crochet in 3rd chain from hook and in each chain across—21 stitches at the end of this row.
Rows 2–16 Chain 2, turn, half double crochet in each stitch across. Change to B in last stitch of Row 16.
Rows 18–32 With B, repeat Row 2. Change to C in last stitch of Row 32.
Rows 33–48 With C, repeat Row 2. Change to A in last stitch of Row 48.
Rows 49–64 With A, repeat Row 2. Change to B in last stitch of Row 64.
Rows 65–80 With B, repeat Row 2.
Fasten off.

PANEL II
Make same as Panel I, working 16 rows of each color in the following order: C, A, B, C, A.

PANEL III
Make same as Panel I, working 16 rows of each color in the following order: B, C, A, B, C.

PANEL IV
Make same as Panel I.

FINISHING
Following Assembly Diagram, sew long edges of Panels together, changing yarn color as needed so that the sewing yarn color matches the yarn in one of the Panels. Weave in ends.

Assembly Diagram

PANEL I	PANEL II	PANEL III	PANEL IV
B	A	C	B
A	C	B	A
C	B	A	C
B	A	C	B
A	C	B	A

homegrown afghan

YARN
Lion Brand® HOMESPUN® (Art. #792)
- 3 skeins #412 Pearls (A)
- 3 skeins #381 Barley (B)
- 3 skeins #407 Painted Desert (C) or colors of your choice

HOOK
- Lion Brand® crochet hook size P/15 (10 mm) or size to obtain gauge

NOTIONS
- Lion Brand® large-eyed blunt needle

ABBREVIATIONS
ch = chain
hdc = half double crochet
rnd(s) = round(s)
RS = right side
Sl st = slip stitch
st(s) = stitch(es)

FINISHED MEASUREMENTS
About 39 x 39 in. (99 x 99 cm)

GAUGES
- 6 hdc = about 4 in. (10 cm).
- One Square = 13 x 13 in. (33 x 33 cm) square.

BE SURE TO CHECK YOUR GAUGES.

When you match the gauge in a pattern, your project will be the size specified in the pattern and the materials specified in the pattern will be sufficient. If it takes you fewer stitches and rows to match the gauge, try using a smaller size hook; if more stitches and rows, try a larger size hook.

NOTES
1. Nine Squares are crocheted, then sewn together to make Afghan.
2. Yarn color is changed on every other row.
3. Instructions are given to fasten off the old color when changing yarn color. If you prefer, carry unused color along side edge of work. Then, when sewing Squares together, be sure to include the side with the carried yarn strands in a seam.

SQUARE 1 (MAKE 5)
With B, ch 21.
Row 1 (RS) Hdc in 3rd ch from hook (beginning ch counts as first hdc) and in each ch across—20 hdc at the end of this row.
Row 2 With B, ch 2 (counts as first hdc in this row and in all following rows), turn, hdc in each st across. Fasten off B.
Row 3 With RS facing, join A with sl st in first st, ch 2, hdc in each st across.
Row 4 With A, ch 2, turn, hdc in each st across. Fasten off A.
Row 5 With RS facing, join B with sl st in first st, ch 2, hdc in each st across.
Row 6 With B, ch 2, turn, hdc in each st across. Fasten off B.
Rows 7–14 Rep Rows 3–6 two more times.
Note There should be 4 stripes of B and 3 stripes of A.
Fasten off.

SQUARE 2 (MAKE 4)
Work same as Square 1, using C instead of B.

FINISHING
Following Assembly Diagram, sew Squares into 3 strips of 3 Squares each. Sew strips together to make Afghan.
Weave in ends.

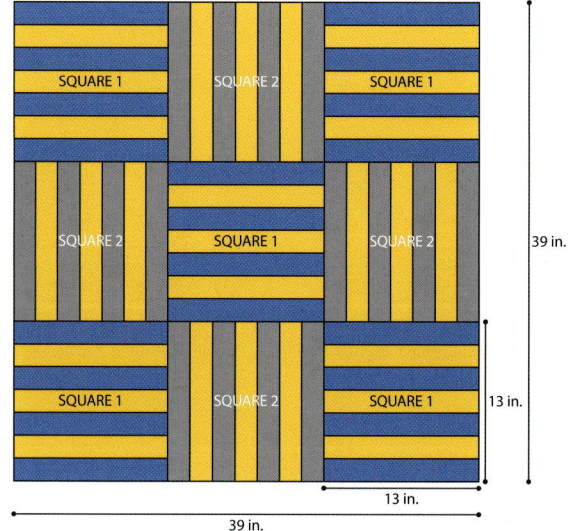

Assembly Diagram

november nights afghan

YARN
Lion Brand® HOMESPUN® (Art. #790)
- 3 skeins #336 Barrington (A)
- 2 skeins #407 Painted Desert (B)
- 2 skeins #408 Wild Fire (C)
- 2 skeins #412 Pearls (D) or colors of your choice

HOOK
- Lion Brand® crochet hook size K/10.5 (6.5 mm) *or size to obtain gauge*

NOTIONS
- Lion Brand® large-eyed blunt needle

ABBREVIATIONS
ch = chain
hdc = half double crochet
rep = repeat
rnd(s) = round(s)
sl st = slip stitch
st(s) = stitch(es)

FINISHED MEASUREMENTS
About 44 x 52 in. (112 x 132 cm)

GAUGES
- 10 hdc and 8 rows = 4 in. (10 cm).
- One Block measures about 8 x 8 in. (20.5 x 20.5 cm).

BE SURE TO CHECK YOUR GAUGES.

When you match the gauge in a pattern, your project will be the size specified in the pattern and the materials specified in the pattern will be sufficient. If it takes you fewer stitches and rows to match the gauge, try using a smaller hook; if more stitches and rows, try a larger hook.

NOTES
1 Afghan is made from 30 identical Blocks.
2 Following the Assembly Diagram, Blocks are sewn into strips, then strips are sewn together to make Afghan. Turning the Blocks in different directions, following the diagram, creates the pattern on the Afghan.
3 Border is crocheted around the outside edge of the completed Afghan.
4 To change color, work last st of old color to last yarn over. Yarn over with new color and draw through all loops to complete st. Fasten off old color.

BLOCKS (MAKE 30)
With A, ch 22.
Row 1 Hdc in 3rd ch from hook (beginning ch does not count as a st) and in each ch across—20 hdc at the end of this row.
Rows 2–4 Ch 2 (does not count as a st), turn, hdc in each st across.
Change to B.
Rows 5–8 With B, rep Row 2 four times.
Change to C.
Rows 9–12 With C, rep Row 2 four times.
Change to D.
Rows 13–16 With D, rep Row 2 four times.
Fasten off.

FINISHING
Note The arrow on each Block in the diagram points from first row to last. Sew Blocks together turned in the directions shown on the diagram. Following Assembly Diagram, sew Blocks into 5 strips of 6 Blocks each. Sew strips together to make Afghan.

Border
Rnd 1 From right side, join A with a sl st anywhere along outer edge of Afghan, sl st evenly around entire outer edge of Afghan; join with sl st in first sl st.
Rnds 2–5 Ch 2, hdc in each st around, working 3 hdc in each corner; join with sl st in first hdc.
Fasten off.
Weave in ends.

november nights afghan

Assembly Diagram

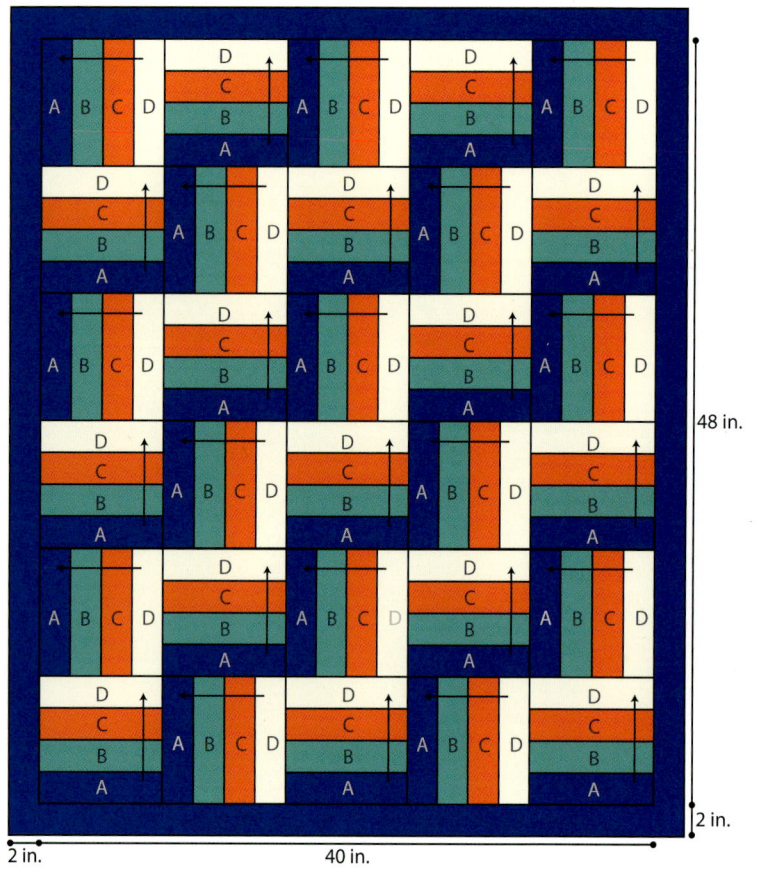

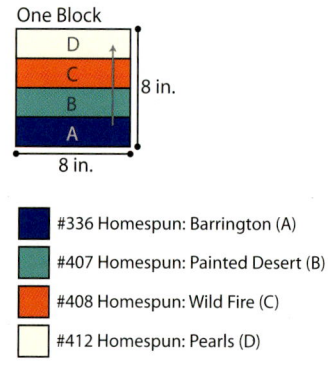

One Block

- #336 Homespun: Barrington (A)
- #407 Homespun: Painted Desert (B)
- #408 Homespun: Wild Fire (C)
- #412 Homespun: Pearls (D)

country colors afghan

YARN
Lion Brand® HOMESPUN® (Art. #790)
- 3 skeins #336 Barrington (A)
- 2 skeins #407 Painted Desert (B)
- 2 skeins #408 Wild Fire (C)
- 2 skeins #412 Pearls (D) or colors of your choice

HOOK
- Lion Brand® crochet hook size K/10.5 (6.5 mm) *or size to obtain gauge*

NOTIONS
- Lion Brand® large-eyed blunt needle

ABBREVIATIONS
ch = chain
hdc = half double crochet
rnd(s) = round(s)
sc = single crochet
sl st = slip stitch
st(s) = stitch(es)

FINISHED MEASUREMENTS
About 34 x 50 in. (86.5 x 127 cm)

GAUGE
10 sc and 10 rows = 4 in. (10 cm).
BE SURE TO CHECK YOUR GAUGE.

When you match the gauge in a pattern, your project will be the size specified in the pattern and the materials specified in the pattern will be sufficient. If it takes you fewer stitches and rows to match the gauge, try using a smaller size hook; if more stitches and rows, try a larger size hook.

NOTES
1 Afghan is made from 6 identical Blocks which are made up of a Center Square and color Strips. Blocks are sewn together and Border worked around the entire outer edge.
2 To change color, work last st of old color to last yarn over. Yarn over with new color and draw through all loops on hook to complete st. Proceed with new color. Fasten off old color.

BLOCK (MAKE 6)
Center Square
With A, ch 11.
Row 1 Sc in 2nd ch from hook and in each ch across—10 sc at the end of this row.
Rows 2–10 Ch 1, turn, sc in each sc across; change to B in last st of Row 10.

Strip I
Row 1 With B, ch 1, turn, sc in each sc across.
Rows 2–5 Ch 1, turn, sc in each sc across. Do not fasten off.

Strip II
Row 1 With B, do not turn, ch 1, work 15 sc evenly across side edge of Strip I and Center Square—15 sc.
Rows 2–5 Ch 1, turn, sc in each sc across; change to C in last st of Row 5.

Strip III
Row 1 With C, do not turn, ch 1, work 15 sc evenly across side edge of Strip II and next edge of Center Square—15 sc.
Rows 2–5 Ch 1, turn, sc in each sc across. Do not fasten off.

Strip IV
Row 1 With C, do not turn, work 20 sc evenly across side edge of Strip III, next edge of Center Square and side edge of Strip I— 20 sc.
Rows 2–5 Ch 1, turn, sc in each sc across; change to D in last st of Row 5.

Strip V
Row 1 With D, do not turn, ch 1, work 20 sc evenly across side edge of Strip IV, last row of Strip I and side edge of Strip II—20 sc.
Rows 2–5 Ch 1, turn, sc in each sc across. Do not fasten off.

country colors afghan

Strip VI
Row 1 With D, do not turn, work 25 sc evenly across side edge of Strip V, last row of Strip II, and side edge of Strip III—25 sc.
Rows 2–5 Ch 1, turn, sc in each sc across; change to E in last st of Row 5.

Strip VII
Row 1 With E, do not turn, ch 1, work 25 sc evenly across side edge of Strip VI, last row of Strip III and side edge of Strip IV—25 sc.
Rows 2–5 Ch 1, turn, sc in each sc across. Do not fasten off.

Strip VIII
Row 1 With E, do not turn, work 30 sc evenly across side edge of Strip VII, last row of Strip IV, and side edge of Strip V—30 sc.
Rows 2–5 Ch 1, turn, sc in each sc across; change to F in last st of Row 5.

Strip IX
Row 1 With F, do not turn, ch 1, work 30 sc evenly across side edge of Strip VIII, last row of Strip V and side edge of Strip VI—30 sc.
Rows 2–5 Ch 1, turn, sc in each sc across. Do not fasten off.

Strip X
Row 1 With F, do not turn, work 35 sc evenly across side edge of Strip IX, last row of Strip VI, and side edge of Strip VII—35 sc.
Rows 2–5 Ch 1, turn, sc in each sc across; change to G in last st of Row 5.

Strip XI
Row 1 With G, do not turn, ch 1, work 35 sc evenly across side edge of Strip X, last row of Strip VII and side edge of Strip VIII—35 sc.
Rows 2–5 Ch 1, turn, sc in each sc across. Do not fasten off.

Strip XII
Row 1 With G, do not turn, work 40 sc evenly across side edge of Strip XI, last row of Strip VIII, and side edge of Strip IX—40 sc.
Rows 2–5 Ch 1, turn, sc in each sc across. Fasten off.

FINISHING
With Strip IX of each Block at top, arrange Blocks into 3 rows of 2 Blocks each and sew together. See Assembly Diagram.

Border
Rnd 1 From right side, join A with sc anywhere in outer edge of Afghan, sc evenly around entire outer edge, working 3 sc in each corner; join with sl st in first sc. Fasten off.
Rnd 2 With G, repeat Rnd 1. Fasten off.
Weave in ends.

Assembly Diagram

city block afghan

YARN
Lion Brand® HOMESPUN® THICK & QUICK® (Art. #792)
- 1 skein #436 Claret (A)
- 1 skein #421 Purple Haze (B)
- 1 skein #407 Painted Desert (C)
- 1 skein #410 Herb Garden (D)
- 1 skein #412 Pearls (E)
- 1 skein #381 Barley (F) or colors of your choice

HOOK
- Lion Brand® crochet hook size P/15 (10 mm) *or size to obtain gauge*

NOTIONS
- Lion Brand® large-eyed blunt needle

ABBREVIATIONS
beg = begin(ning)(s)
ch = chain
hdc = half double crochet
rem = remain(ing)(s)
rep = repeat
rnd = round
RS = right side
sc = single crochet
sl st = slip st
st(s) = stitch(es)

FINISHED MEASUREMENTS
About 48 x 48 in. (122 x 122 cm)

GAUGE
6 hdc and 5 rows = 4 in. (10 cm).
BE SURE TO CHECK YOUR GAUGE.

When you match the gauge in a pattern, your project will be the size specified in the pattern and the materials specified in the pattern will be sufficient. If it takes you fewer stitches and rows to match the gauge, try using a smaller size hook; if more stitches and rows, try a larger size hook.

STITCH GLOSSARYS
hdc2tog (hdc 2 sts together) (Yarn over, insert hook in next st and draw up a loop) twice, yarn over and draw through all 5 loops on hook—1 st decreased.

hdc3tog (hdc 3 sts together) (Yarn over, insert hook in next st and draw up a loop) 3 times, yarn over and draw through all 7 loops on hook—2 sts decreased.

NOTES
1 Afghan is made from 4 identical Blocks. Blocks are sewn together and then Border is worked around entire outer edge.
2 Each Block is worked diagonally beg at one corner. Because of the diagonal construction each Block may not be perfectly square when finished. Seaming will make the Blocks more square.
3 To change color, work last st of old color to last yarn over. Yarn over with new color and draw through all loops on hook to complete the st. Proceed with new color. Fasten off old color.

COLOR SEQUENCE
Work 2 rows each with A, *B, C, D, E, F, E, D, C, B, A; rep from * once more for a total of 42 rows.

BLOCK (MAKE 4)
With A, ch 3.
Row 1 Work 3 hdc in 3rd ch from hook (beg ch does not count as a st)—3 hdc at the end of this row.
Row 2 Ch 2 (does not count as a st on this row or on any of the following rows), turn, 2 hdc in first st, hdc in each st across to last st, 2 hdc in last st—5 hdc.
Change to B.
Rows 3 and 4 With C, rep Row 2 twice—9 hdc at the end of Row 4.
Change to C. Continue to change color at the end of every other row, following Color Sequence, until Block is complete.
Rows 6–21 Rep Row 2 nineteen more times—43 hdc at the end of Row 21.
Row 22 Ch 2, turn, hdc2tog, hdc in each st across to last 2 sts, hdc2tog—41 sts.
Row 23–41 Rep Row 22 until only 3 sts rem.
Row 42 Ch 2, turn, hdc3tog.
Fasten off.

city block afghan

FINISHING
With Row 1 of each Block at center, sew Blocks together.

Border
Rnd 1 From RS, join F with sc anywhere in outer edge of Afghan, work sc evenly spaced around entire outside edge, working 3 sc in each corner; join with sl st in first sc. Fasten off.

Rnd 2 From RS, join A with sl st in any st, ch 2 (does not count as a st), hdc in each st around, working 3 hdc in each corner; join with sl st in top of beg ch. Fasten off.

Rnd 3 With F, rep Rnd 2.
Fasten off.
Weave in ends.